# THE PIANIST'S FIRST MUSIC MAKING

## BOOK II.

# TOBIAS MATTHAY

### AND

# FELIX SWINSTEAD

# Read & Co.

Copyright © 2021 Read & Co. Books

This edition is published by Read & Co. Books,
an imprint of Read & Co.

This book is copyright and may not be reproduced or copied in any
way without the express permission of the publisher in writing.

British Library Cataloguing-in-Publication Data
A catalogue record for this book is available
from the British Library.

Read & Co. is part of Read Books Ltd.
For more information visit
www.readandcobooks.co.uk

# Tobias Matthay

Tobias Augustus Matthay was born on 19th February 1858, in Clapham, Surrey, England. He was an English pianist, teacher and composer.

Matthay's parents originally came from northern Germany and eventually became naturalised British subjects. He studied composition at the 'Royal Academy of Music' (London) under Sir William Sterndale Bennett and Arthur Sullivan, and piano with William Dorrell and Walter Macfarren. Matthay served as a sub-professor there from 1876 to 1880, and became an assistant professor of pianoforte in 1880, before being promoted to professor in 1884.

Alongside Frederick Corder and John Blackwood McEwen (both composers and music teachers), he founded the Society of British Composers in 1905. This organisation was established with the aim of protecting the interests of British composers and to provide publication, promotion and performance opportunities. It was disbanded thirteen years later, in 1918. Matthay remained at the Royal Academy of Music until 1925, when he was forced to resign because McEwen – his former student who was then the Academy's Principal – publicly attacked his teaching.

In 1903, after over a decade of observation, analysis, and experimentation, Matthay published *The Act of Touch*, an encyclopaedic volume that influenced piano pedagogy throughout the English-speaking world. So many students were soon in quest of his insights that two years later he opened the Tobias Matthay Pianoforte School, first in Oxford Street, then in 1909 relocating to Wimpole Street, where it remained for the next thirty years. He soon became known for his teaching principles that stressed proper piano touch and analysis of arm movements. He wrote several additional books on piano technique that brought him international recognition, and in 1912 he published *Musical Interpretation*, a widely read book that analyzed the principles of effective musicianship.

Many of Matthay's pupils went on to define a school of twentieth century English pianism, including York Bowen, Myra Hess, Clifford Curzon, Moura Lympany, Eunice Norton, Lytle Powell, Irene Scharrer, Lilias Mackinnon, Guy Jonson, Vivian Langrish and Harriet Cohen. He was also the teacher of Canadian pianist Harry Dean, English composer Arnold Bax and English conductor Ernest Read.

In his private life, Matthay married Jessie (née Kennedy) in 1893, the sister of Marjory Kennedy-Fraser (the Scottish singer, composer and arranger). She sadly died in 1937.

Tobias Matthay died at his country home, High Marley, near Haslemere, on 15th December 1945. He was eighty-seven years old.

# THE PIANIST'S
# FIRST MUSIC MAKING

FOR USE IN CONJUNCTION WITH

TOBIAS MATTHAY'S

## "THE CHILD'S FIRST STEPS"

IN

PIANOFORTE PLAYING

MUSIC COMPOSED BY

# FELIX SWINSTEAD

PREFACE AND DIRECTIONS

BY

# TOBIAS MATTHAY

BOOK II

# CONTENTS.

## BOOK I.

## BOOK II.

# THE PIANIST'S FIRST MUSIC MAKING.

## BOOK II.

---

## SECTION VII.

### ROTATION STUDY.

#### THE EMPLOYMENT OF ALL FIVE FINGERS ALTERNATELY.

In *Section IV.*, Step IV., page 13, of Book I., you learnt to help the thumb and little finger by alternately exerting and relaxing the forearm "twistingly"—that is *rotationally*. You must now learn to give this same *rotatory* help to all the other fingers when required.

First read and study all that is said under *Step XII.* of the " Child's First Steps "; also practise carefully, over and over again, the little preparatory exercises there given on pages 10 and 11.*

You can then learn to play Examples Nos. 21 to 24, given here.

It would be best to learn these at first *without their chord accompaniments*, asking your teacher to play these with you. Afterwards, learn to play these accompaniments yourself.

To enable you better to understand the *legato*, which is here required, carefully study the directions of *Step X.* of the " Child's First Steps." You will see, that to make the *legato* you must allow a very slight weight to remain *resting on the keyboard* all through such *legato* passage. This *compels* your fingers to hold each note down till the next, thus connecting the sounds. The weight must be quite light, only just enough, and you must *pass this weight on* from finger to finger, just as you do the weight of your body when you walk along *nicely*, without lurching from side to side.†

---

\* The " Child's First Steps," Tobias Matthay. (Joseph Williams, Ltd.)

† Later on, when you are a more advanced student, you will also learn another form of *legato*—the " artificial " *legato*, where the fingers hold their notes without being thus *compelled* to do so by weight.

No 21.            IN WINTER.           FELIX SWINSTEAD.
PUPIL.
Allegretto

No 22.           DOLL'S DANCE.        FELIX SWINSTEAD.
PUPIL.
Allegretto.

No 23.           PLAYFELLOWS.         FELIX SWINSTEAD.
TEACHER.
Allegretto.

No 24.           AUTUMN SONG.         FELIX SWINSTEAD.
TEACHER.
Allegretto.

PUPIL. L.H. also R.H. seperately.

Examples No. 25 to 27—continue the same lesson. They are a little more advanced; you can try them now, or come back to them a little later on. You can play the accompanying chords yourself, or may ask your teacher to play these for you at first.

You can also use the treble part for *left hand study*, having someone else to play the Bass underneath your part, as a "Secondo."

**N? 25.**       HAPPINESS.       FELIX SWINSTEAD.

Nᵒ 26 PUPIL.                           CONTENTMENT.*

* The pupil will first learn the quaver portion for R.H., and also the quaver portion for L.H., the teacher crossing over to play the accompaniments.   Later on the pupil can play the piece as a Solo.

No. 27.★                          JOY.                    FELIX SWINSTEAD.

Allegro con spirito.

PUPIL.

PUPIL.

* This piece should be treated as the last one, the teacher at first playing the minim accompaniments.

## Nº 28.    FROSTY MORN.

FELIX SWINSTEAD.

**PUPIL.** As Duet at first, Solo afterwards.

Allegro con spirito.

## CARRILLON

No. 29.

PUPIL. As a Duet at first, Solo afterwards.

FELIX SWINSTEAD.

No 30.

## A DREARY DAY.

As a Duet at first.
Allegretto.

FELIX SWINSTEAD.

# A SUNNY DAY.

**No 31.**
As a Duet at first.
Allegretto.

FELIX SWINSTEAD.

# SECTION VIII.

## ROTATION STUDY.

### ITS APPLICATION TO ADJACENT FINGERS.

You must now learn how the rotatory help must be given when you play the remaining *next-door fingers* in succession—2, 3 and 3, 4. Here again refer to "Child's First Steps,"—to *Step XIII* (page 11).

First practise Ex. No. 10, on page 11, of "Child's First Steps," and after that take the little Duets here, Nos. 32 and 33 That is, use these as Duets at first. Afterwards play the accompaniments yourself.

The point to realize, is, that the rotational help is always given *from* the finger last used *towards* the next finger. In examples 32 and 33 the fingering has been grouped together, to show this to you.

Having thus learned to give the correct rotational help to *adjacent* (next-door) fingers, you will then be able to start practising *FIVE FINGER Exercises* of all kinds; and you will now be able to derive benefit from them, provided you always remember the lesson learnt in this section—*Section VIII*. A simple example is given (No. 11) on page **12 of** "Child's First Steps."†

**Nº 32.**                    **PLAINTIVE TUNE.**                    FELIX SWINSTEAD.

As a Duet at first, as a Solo afterwards.

Tempo di Valse.

---

† A certain number of "Five-finger" exercises—a few—may now be practised without danger of doing actual harm—as would be the case if the rotary adjustments were not understood. It is indeed well to do *some* practice of this nature now, so as to gain facility in this respect. Also, from here onwards become available the Duet examples of Mrs. Curwen's *Grade I*, both those of the first edition, by John Kinross, and those of the later edition by Felix Swinstead. Moreover, to keep the pupil's musical imagination active, other pieces should also be taken in hand, such as those mentioned in the preface to this work.

No 33.

THE 'CELLO PLAYER.

FELIX SWINSTEAD.

As a Duet at first, as a Solo afterwards.
Tempo di Valse.

# SECTION IX.

## LEARNING TO TURN THE THUMB UNDER AND THE FINGERS OVER.

After having gained some little "knack" in the playing of complete five-finger positions, the next step is to combine *portions* of these five-finger positions so as to form the Scale. A scale consists of two incomplete five-finger positions, a longer and shorter one. The longer one consists of *four* notes (and fingers), and the shorter one of only *three* notes (and fingers); and both fingering *positions* begin with the thumb. Thus you have the position 1234 and the position 123. These positions, however, do not occur at the same places in all the scales; they occur at *different* places, that is why you have to learn the scale fingerings; and these you must learn so that you can better choose your fingering in pieces.

Now these two positions must be nicely *joined together*; therefore, before you can try to play a scale, you must learn to turn the thumb *under* the fingers, and also the fingers *over* the thumb. When the scale moves from the centre towards the end of the keyboard, you have to turn your thumb under, so as to join the fingering groups; but when the scale moves the other way, then you have to turn a finger over the thumb, for the same purpose.

Here study the directions and exercises given in Section XVIII (page 15) "The Child's First Steps" for turning the thumb under, and those on page 16, for turning the fingers over. Be careful to note when you turn a finger over the thumb, that the rotative help from the Forearm is *towards the little-finger side of the hand*, and not, (as you might expect) towards the thumb-side of the hand. Unless you learn this correctly at once, you will always play every scale and arpeggio very clumsily at those "turning-over" places. Allow the hand to move freely from the wrist, to help the thumb and fingers and arm in their required lateral movements.*

---

* "Lateral," or horizontal, here refers to movements up or down the keyboard.

**No 34.**
As a Duet at first.
Grave.

SOLEMN PRELUDE.

FELIX SWINSTEAD.

**No 35.**
As a Duet at first.
Tempo di Valse.

VALSE TUNE.

FELIX SWINSTEAD.

**No 36.**
As Duet at first.
Allegro.

IN A HURRY.

FELIX SWINSTEAD.

No. 37.

IN THE HARBOUR.

FELIX SWINSTEAD.

As a Duet at first.

Allegretto.

No. 38.

THE BANSHEE.

FELIX SWINSTEAD.

As a Duet at first.

Allegro con spirito.

No. 39.

AMONG THE HEATHER.

FELIX SWINSTEAD.

As Duet at first.

Allegretto.

# SCALE PREPARATION.

## PREAMBLE.

The teaching of the Scale is usually begun wrongly, because the issues have been confused. Learning to *read* the notes of a scale and learning to *play* a scale have been mistaken as one single problem, whereas they really are two quite distinct problems. Because of this mistake, C major has been given to the pupil as his first scale. True, it is the easiest to *read*; but it is indeed one of the hardest to *play* properly. There are no landmarks in it such as the other scales offer, with their black digits contrasting with the white ones in key-level. Being all of one level, C major, besides, does not offer us the same facility in turning the thumb under, or the fingers over, which other tonalities, with black keys, offer us. C major, also, is not so likely to prompt the best position of the fingers and of the hand laterally. The very easiest scales to play on a key-board instrument are the three tonalities which employ *all* the black digits; viz.: D flat, B and F sharp major. These are more likely to prompt us correctly in these respects, since the thumb here falls naturally into its right position. Turning over, and under, is also facilitated.

CHOPIN used *B* major as the first scale with pupils, but I advocate taking *F* sharp major for the player-beginner, where possible, as it suggests better harmonic combinations than most of the other scales, when taken by contrary motion—as a scale should logically be taken at first. Also, it gives us both *fingering positions*, with the identical *kind* of digits in the two hands (white and black), when taken by contrary motion, and starting on *B* and *E* sharp in the right and left hand, respectively. Thus, in the right hand, for the "long" fingering position, we start on the *white* key *E* sharp, followed by three black keys (or digits), while the "short" fingering position begins with the thumb on the *white* key *B* followed by *two* fingers again on black keys; the left hand has corresponding white and black keys to play, starting the two fingering positions with the thumb on *B* and *E* sharp, respectively.

The difficulty of reading or learning the notes of the key of *F* sharp is greatly exaggerated. As its notation has *every* note raised a semitone by a sharp, except *B*, it is not really more difficult to remember than *G* major with its single sharp, and all other notes un-sharpened. *F* sharp major is the key with *one natural*, that is all.

Even if it does give a little more trouble at first, it is worth this, seeing all its advantages for a first scale. And with a child, the teacher will have to "show the notes" at first, anyway.

Certain hands, of very small size, *may* however find the slight extension of the fingers on to the black keys a little irksome, although so much easier a position for a hand somewhat less small. To meet this case I have added also a "first example" in C major. But *F* sharp should be taken wherever possible.

Moreover, to carry out the logical succession of difficulties in *performance* (not difficulty in *spelling* or *reading*), scales should first be learnt by *contrary* motion—for the same reason that the practice of five-finger exercises is more likely to lead to good playing if at first taken also by contrary motion, as seen in Steps XII, XIII and XIV, of "Child's First Steps." The reason, as already pointed out, is that we are more likely to acquire the correct rotational changes of the forearm when these are at first used in *similar* direction, than if we try to learn them, with opposite requirements in the two hands, in this respect.

Therefore, also, great care must be taken with regard to Rotation, when the scales at last are taken by *similar* motion. Stiffness, rotationally, is indeed the most common technical blunder, and it affects all playing—agility as well as accuracy of colouring. Moreover, it is precisely in the earliest stages of studentship that bad habits in this respect are formed, with all their heart-breaking results afterwards. Too much care, therefore, cannot be lavished to ensure that the forearm rotational changes are correctly learned at the very beginning. See "Child's First Steps" pages 4, and 9 to 14.

# SECTION X.

## SCALE-PREPARATION.

### LEARNING THE FINGER-GROUPING.

After having practised some of the last exercises, for turning the thumb under, **and** the fingers over, Nos. (34 to 39) you can now learn further to prepare yourself for the scale. Realize, that an octave of scale consists always of the *two groups of notes and fingers*, the "long" group (thumb with three fingers), and the "short" group (thumb **and** two fingers).

"Learning the notes" of any particular scale implies that you must make yourself remember *how* these two fingering-*groups*, the one short and the other long, are to belong to the respective two groups of notes on the keyboard—*with their respective* SOUNDS, thus forming the particular scale.

Ask your teacher now to show you these two groups of notes and fingers, for **the scale** of *F* sharp; this, although it looks hard, is the easiest to play at first.

These two groups for the scale of *F* sharp are as follows:

**No. 40.**              THE SCALE OF F SHARP.

Right Hand fingering and notes.

and   Left Hand fingering and notes.

R.H.

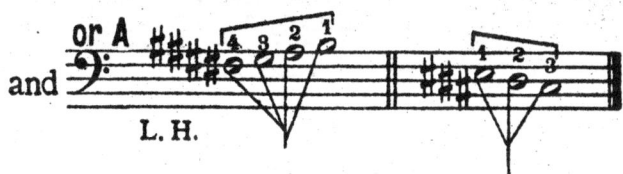
and   L. H.

First place *all* the fingers belonging to a group on its required keys (or digits) as **at** (A) No. 40. You need not sound them yet. Just notice how they look and feel to you in these *four* positions—two for the right hand and two for the left hand. Then take (B), next page. Here you will *sound* the notes of each group backwards and forwards, so **that** you can *hear* how they each sound, and thus make yourself remember which *sounds*, which digits, and which *fingers* belong together for this scale of *F* sharp which you **are** trying to learn. Of course sound the notes carefully, as you have learned in the **earlier** exercises. Insist on making the sounds *when* you want them, *how* you want them, **and** always *quite easily*.

---

* The Examples 40 to 46 are by Tobias Matthay.

# THE HOUSE THAT JACK BUILT.

Next take (C). Here you have to sound the two groups one after the other, the "short" one and then the "long" one. Do not try just now to connect these groups.

Now practise (D). Here you play the same groups as in (C), but they must now be *connected*, or joined together by carefully turning the 4th (ring) finger over the thumb—as you have already learned to do. Take care to remember, when you turn the 4th finger over the thumb, that the arm must be free, *rotationally*, towards the little-finger side of of your hand.* Be careful, also, that you do not turn the hand over with a *jerk*.

Notice next, when you turn the finger over the thumb as in this last exercise, that you naturally *turn the hand* laterally in the same direction as the finger.† That is, you turn the hand slightly *inwards*. This, indeed, is the position of the hand, "laterally" for playing all scales in single notes, such as you are now learning. Leave the hand thus turned "inwards" from the wrist. Do not turn it back, this will enable you to turn the fingers over, and the thumb under, without any further movement of the hand itself.

Re-read also (very carefully) what is said on page 17, " Child's First Steps " as to the practice of the scale.

After having learned to do these things with some ease, you can now take exercises *E, F, G,* and finally, *H.*

---

* See page 17 "Child's First Steps."
† See note, bottom of page 15.

You may even, at last, play all these (*E* to *H*) without stopping—making them into a little piece.

All the time, however, be sure to play them as musical *movements* or progressions—feel the little figures move (walk) towards the places shown by the arrows. In fact, always make everything you play sound like music; even such exercises as these. Recall what is said in the "Foreword" to "Child's First Steps"—or better, read it again.

Nos. I and J offer the same practice as the last, but they are a little more difficult.

So far you have only taken the scale *going towards you.* That is the easiest way to begin. You must now learn, just as easily, to play the scale moving the opposite way— *away* from you.

The same advice applies as for all the last exercises. You must however, be careful to keep the hands still turned slightly "inwards," although you now have to move your arm *away* from you—towards the ends of the keyboard, instead of towards the middle, as you have done so far. If not careful, you will most likely let the wrist turn inwards; instead of keeping it turned *outwards*—"in front" of the moving scale, as it were.

While learning these exercises, K to N, you may also practise the Duet No. 47, and others.

You must now learn to play the scale with both hands moving in the *same* direction. Practise the left hand alone first, as in Example *O*; then together as in Example *P*. It seems easier to read the same notes in both hands, and so it is; but unless careful, you will *play* it really less well than you have done while playing it by contrary motion. The reason is, again, that so long as you play by contrary motion, most of the forearm-rotation changes are in the *same* direction, and that is easier to do rightly. When you play the scale by similar motion these changes, however, will mostly occur in the *opposite* direction. This may lead to your playing stiffly, instead of easily; and when you play "stiffly" then you cannot make music. Bear in mind, therefore, all you have learnt in *Step XII,* and the exercises in illustration of "Forearm Rotation."

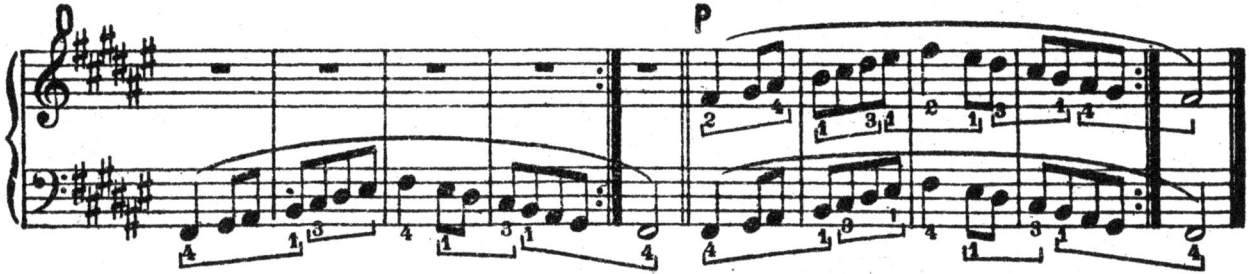

If you find the scale of *F* sharp too difficult to manage, because your hand may be **too** small to reach the black keys easily, then you must first practise in *C* major. But it is far better to try to master *F* sharp first, if you can reach the notes without too much effort, because *F* sharp is more easy to play *well* than *C* major. Exercises, Set No. 41 (A to G) will help you to learn the scale of *C*. The same advice applies that has been given for Set No. 1, so it need not be repeated here.

## No 41.          THE SCALE OF C MAJOR.

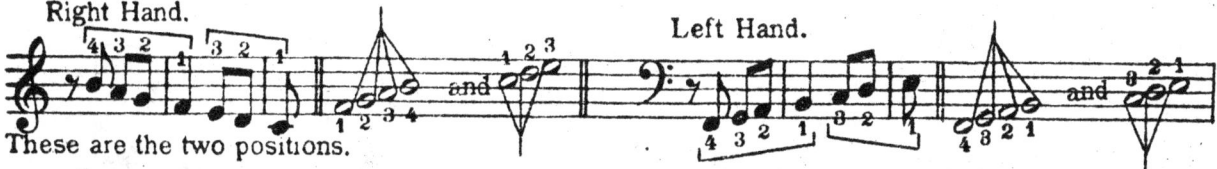

These are the two positions.

★ Both thumbs on the same C.
Be careful of the turning over of the 3rd finger.

N.B. The 5th is here used as an 'extra' finger, in place of the thumb.

As further preparation for scale-playing, practise the following Set of Examples, Sets Nos. 42 to 46.

These keys are chosen, because they enable you to play with the *same groups of fingers* in both hands. That is easier at first than playing different finger-groups together.

Remember all that has been said about *Set 40*, because it applies all the time, also in these new keys.

No. 42.    FOR SCALE OF E FLAT.

No. 43.    FOR SCALE OF A FLAT.

FOR SCALE OF G.

*The correct fingering, not the orthodox!

FOR SCALE OF E.

FOR SCALE OF A.

Again, the proper fingering, not the "orthodox!" *

* The fingering here used for the left hand of *A* and *G* major is unorthodox. It is however, the only logically correct fingering. Manifestly, it is easier to turn the thumb under (or the reverse process) *with a finger or a black key*, than with a finger on a *white* key.

The scale of *D* major, also, for the same reason, should be fingered with the thumb on *B* and *E* in the

You can now learn to play all the other scales. Your teacher, or any scale Book will give you the fingering for these.

But before trying to learn any new scale, always learn the *groupings* first. Place each hand in turn *on the keys* of the *long group*, and on the notes of the short group. Thoroughly realize *where each fingering group* lies on its note-group. Then sound the notes of each group backwards and forwards, each hand separately, so as to remember which *sounds* are played with each group of fingers. Thus you will learn the fingerings of the scales in the quickest way.

---

left hand, and not, as usually mis-fingered. *F* minor in its harmonic form, should similarly have the left hand thumb on *G* and *C*. It is, however, perhaps best to break this rule in the case of the left hand fingering of the minor scales of *C*, *F*, *E* flat, *G* and *A*, in their harmonic form. Following the rule here, would give a rather uncomfortable extension between certain fingers; therefore perhaps it is here best to adhere to the "orthodox" fingering. The orthodox *right hand* fingerings of nearly all the scales happen to be in accordance with the rule mentioned; but in the case of *C* minor (harmonic) the right hand thumb might perhaps be found easier on *B* natural, and on *F*.

No doubt, the mis-fingerings pointed out have arisen from a desire to render the *memorizing* of the scale fingerings easier, whereas fingering should always be chosen with a view to rendering *good playing* easier.

# SECTION XI.

## THE APPLICATION OF THE SCALE

This does not really come within the province of this book; but a few examples in Duet form follow. Of course, bear in mind all you have just learnt as to scale playing when you work at these examples, and other similar ones. It all applies, indeed, to every piece you learn in the coming years.

No. 47. IN THE CATHEDRAL. FELIX SWINSTEAD.

**N⁰ 48.**      **VALSE.**      FELIX SWINSTEAD.

No. 49.

# THE SWITCHBACK.

FELIX SWINSTEAD.

Allegretto.

No. 50.

# THE RETURN JOURNEY.

FELIX SWINSTEAD.

Allegretto.

No. 51.

FELIX SWINSTEAD.

Allegretto cantabile.

PUPIL.

TEACHER

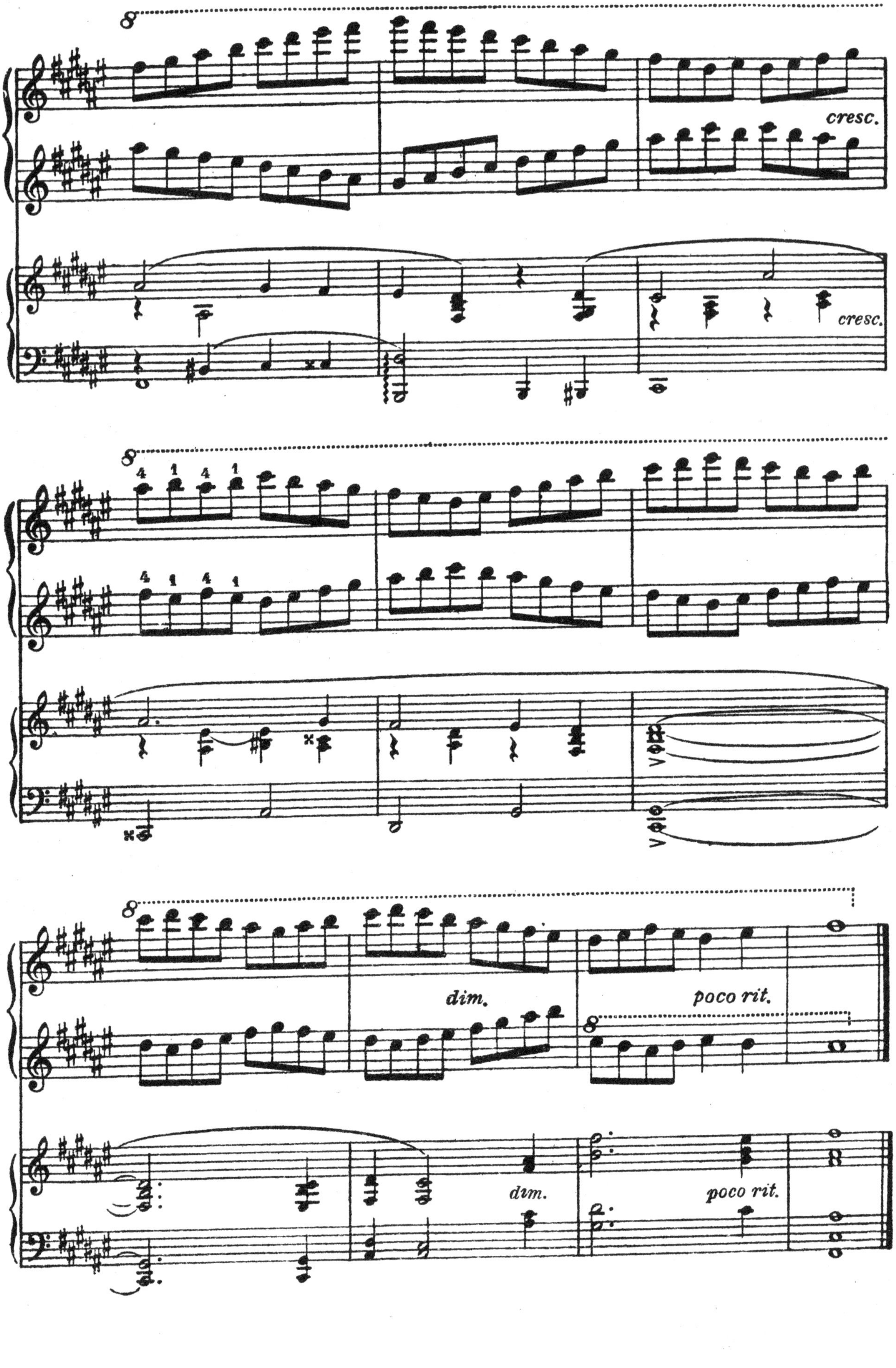
8
cresc.
cresc.
8
4 1 4 1
4 1 4 1
8
dim.
poco rit.
8
dim.
poco rit.

# SECTION XII.

## CODA.

### A FEW WORDS TO THE TEACHER.*

" The teacher of children, to be successful, must proceed on precisely the same lines as those upon which the teacher of the advanced pupil must proceed if he would secure success.

He must explain and *analyse everything*. He must provoke the wish to acquire knowledge, and stimulate the wish for the understanding of everything in every respect.

He must explain fully all the *technical* ways and means, physical and mental, through which we obtain Colouring and Agility; and he must explain, also, all the inexorable laws, and principles implied in successful Interpretation—laws through which we learn *how* to concentrate through rhythmical attention upon the *feeling* of the music.†

Moreover and beyond all this, as I have insisted upon before, and here again insist. all must be explained with intimate reference to music itself.

It must not be explanation for the sake merely of understanding the facts, as such, but it must be explanation given for the sake of helping the pupil to an immediate better-ment of his *musical understanding*, preception, musical outlook, and self-expression, emotionally.

Moreover, we must remember, as I warned the reader of my " Act of Touch "—a good many years ago now—that mastery of a language remains useless as a vehicle for free expression, until its whole mechanism has become semi-automatic. That is, one cannot freely express oneself, until one's knowledge of a language, the ways of applying it, its vocabulary, its grammar, its syntax have all been relegated to that reservoir—that fountain head—or say, that *granary* where we store up all we learn; and where, also, is stored up the mass of experience we inherit from our forebears—I refer to the most important faculty of the artist—his control of the resources of the *sub-conscious* brain.

Now, it is from this storehouse of the widest-reaching judgment, the Sub-consciousness, that, in the end should emanate all our artistic promptings to Speech. The point, therefore, which we must insist upon with every pupil, is, that when it comes to actual playing, to the performance of Music, he must listen to the mandates of his own *sub-conscious* brain.

However careful and painstaking, and analytical all the *necessary preparation*, the actual *performance* of music can be successful only when we insist on allowing our sub-conscious brain to prompt us into the *mood*—as the music passes along. Only if we succeed in this will our playing cease to be mere stuttering mechanics—however clever and finished; only then may it become Art—yes, even with the child ! "

TOBIAS MATTHAY,

HASLEMERE.

*September, 1918.*

---

* From a lecture on Children's Music, first delivered March, 1918.
† See " Musical Interpretation " by Tobias Matthay (Joseph Williams, Ltd.)

www.ingramcontent.com/pod-product-compliance
Lightning Source LLC
Chambersburg PA
CBHW081138090426
42737CB00018B/3359